D1038227

May your dreams
never disappear with age,
but may they continue
as alive and as beautiful as you
with the knowledge that they
will someday come true.

— *Joanne Domenech*

Blue Mountain Arts®

Bestselling Books

By Susan Polis Schutz:

To My Daughter, with Love, on the Important Things in Life
To My Son, with Love
I Love You

100 Things to Always Remember... and One Thing to Never Forget
by Alin Austin

Is It Time to Make a Change?
by Deanna Beisser

Trust in Yourself
by Donna Fargo

To the One Person I Consider to Be My Soul Mate
by D. Pagels

For You, Just Because You're Very Special to Me
by Collin McCarty

Chasing Away the Clouds
by Douglas Pagels

A Lifetime of Love... Poems on the Passages of Life
by Leonard Nimoy

Anthologies:

42 Gifts I'd Like to Give to You
Always Believe in Yourself and Your Dreams
Creeds of Life, Love, & Inspiration
Follow Your Dreams Wherever They Lead You
For You, My Daughter
Friends Are Forever
Friends for Life
I Love You, Mom
I'm Glad You Are My Sister
The Joys and Challenges of Motherhood
The Language of Recovery ...and Living Life One Day at a Time
Life Can Be Hard Sometimes ...but It's Going to Be Okay
Marriage Is a Promise of Love
May You Always Have an Angel by Your Side
Mottos to Live By
Take Each Day One Step at a Time
Teaching and Learning Are Lifelong Journeys
There Is Greatness Within You, My Son
These Are the Gifts I'd Like to Give to You
Think Positive Thoughts Every Day
Thoughts of Friendship
Thoughts to Share with a Wonderful Teenager
To My Child
With God by Your Side ...You Never Have to Be Alone

Don't Ever Give Up Your Dreams

A Blue Mountain Arts®
Collection

Blue Mountain Press™
SPS Studios, Inc., Boulder, Colorado

Copyright © 1983, 2001 by Stephen Schutz and Susan Polis Schutz.

All rights reserved. No part of this publication may be reproduced, stored in a retrieval system or transmitted in any form or by any means, electronic, mechanical, photocopying, recording or otherwise, without the written permission of the publisher.

We wish to thank Susan Polis Schutz for permission to reprint the following poems that appear in this publication: "This life is yours..." and "If you know...." Copyright © 1978 by Continental Publications. And for "Love Your Life," "You Deserve the Best," and "Find happiness in nature...." Copyright © 1982, 1983 by Stephen Schutz and Susan Polis Schutz. All rights reserved.

We wish to thank Donna Fargo for permission to reprint the poems "I Know You Can Make Your Dreams Come True" and "Reach for the Stars, Go for Your Dreams!" in this publication. Copyright © 2001 by PrimaDonna Entertainment Corp. All rights reserved.

Library of Congress Catalog Card Number: 2001001901
ISBN: 0-88396-637-9 (hardcover) — ISBN: 0-88396-183-0 (trade paper)

ACKNOWLEDGMENTS appear on page 64.

Certain trademarks are used under license.

Manufactured in China
First Printing in Hardcover: June 2002

This book is printed on recycled paper.

This book is printed on fine quality, laid embossed, 80 lb. paper. This paper has been specially produced to be acid free (neutral pH) and contains no groundwood or unbleached pulp. It conforms with all the requirements of the American National Standards Institute, Inc., so as to ensure that this book will last and be enjoyed by future generations.

Library of Congress Cataloging-in-Publication Data

Don't ever give up your dreams : a Blue Mountain Arts collection.
p. cm.
ISBN 0-88396-637-9 (alk. paper)
ISBN 0-88396-183-0 (pbk : alk. paper)
1. Self-actualization (Psychology)—Poetry. 2. American poetry—20th century.
3. Success—Poetry. I. Blue Mountain Arts (Firm)
PS595.S45 D66 2001
811'.5080353—dc21

2001001901
CIP

SPS Studios, Inc.

P.O. Box 4549, Boulder, Colorado 80306

Contents

1 Joanne Domenech
7 Shannon M. Lester
8 Donna Fargo
11 amanda pierce
12 Darwin P. Kingsley
13 Laine Parsons
15 Ann Davies
16 Gail Nishimoto
17 Evelyn K. Tharp
19 Susan Polis Schutz
20 Susan Staszewski
21 Donna Wayland
23 Louise Driscoll
24 Susan Polis Schutz
27 Edith Schaffer Lederberg
27 Anonymous
28 Lee Wilkinson
29 Phillips Brooks
31 Edmund O'Neill
32 V. Sukomlin
32 Lin Yutang
33 Prentice Mulford
35 Woodrow Wilson
36 Albert M. Ward
37 Susan Staszewski
39 Helen Keller
39 Linda DuPuy Moore
40 Johnnie Rosenauer
41 Claudia Adrienne Grandi
43 Socrates
43 Debbie Avery
44 D. H. Lawrence
44 James R. Miller
45 Chris Jensen
47 Susan Polis Schutz
48 Linda S. Smith
49 Theophile Gautier
51 amanda pierce
52 Susan Polis Schutz
53 Ida Scott Taylor
55 Michael Rille
56 Kele Daniels
57 Elisa Costanza
59 Susan Polis Schutz
60 Donna Fargo
63 Collin McCarty
64 Acknowledgments

Don't Ever Let Anything Stand in the Way of Your Dreams

Catch the star that holds your destiny —
the one that forever twinkles within your heart
Take advantage of precious opportunities
while they still sparkle before you
Always believe that your ultimate goal
is attainable as long as
you commit yourself to it
Though barriers may sometimes
stand in the way of your dreams
remember that your destiny is hiding behind them
Accept the fact that not everyone
is going to approve of the choices you make
Have faith in your judgment
Catch the star that twinkles in your heart
and it will lead you to your destiny's path
Follow that pathway and uncover the
sweet sunrises that await you
Take pride in your accomplishments
as they are steppingstones to your dreams
Understand that you may make mistakes
but don't let them discourage you
Value your capabilities and talents
for they are what make you truly unique
You are capable of making
your brightest dreams come true
Give your hopes everything you've got
and you will catch the star that holds your destiny

— Shannon M. Lester

I Know You Can Make Your Dreams Come True

I am confident that you can do anything you set your mind to. Whatever hopes you have for your future, I believe you can find a way to make your dreams come true.

Whatever challenges you face in life, I believe you'll turn every experience into something positive. When you have serious questions you need to answer or emotions you need to process, I know that you'll take your time and do the right thing.

Even though there may be times when you'll be dissatisfied with the way things are going in your life, I know you'll learn the lessons you need to learn and eventually make the changes you need to make and move on.

I want you to know that I am always thinking of you, praying for you, and wishing you the best. If you need me to talk to about your concerns, I'm here to support you, just like I know you are for me if I need you.

You are a bright, sweet, thoughtful, and wonderful human being, and I'll always believe in you.

— *Donna Fargo*

Don't Give Up

I know you're going
to make it...
It may take time
and hard work
You may become frustrated
and at times you'll feel
like giving up
Sometimes you may even
wonder if it's really
worth it
But I have confidence in you,
and I know you'll make it
if you try.

— amanda pierce

You have powers you never dreamed of. You can do things you never thought you could do. There are no limitations in what you can do except the limitations in your own mind as to what you cannot do.

Don't think you cannot.

Think you can.

— *Darwin P. Kingsley*

You never know
until you try.
And you never try
unless you <u>really</u> try.
You give it your best shot;
you do the best you can.

And if you've done everything
in your power, and still "fail" —
the truth of the matter is
that you haven't failed at all.

When you reach for your dreams,
no matter what they may be,
you grow from the reaching;
you learn from the trying;
you win from the doing.

— *Laine Parsons*

Learning isn't easy...
frustration tends to set in quickly.
You hurt.
You feel defeated.
You want to give up —
to quit.
You want to walk away
and pretend it doesn't matter.
But you won't,
because you're not a loser —
you're a fighter...

We all have to lose sometimes
before we can win.
We have to cry sometimes
before we can smile.
We have to hurt
before we can be strong.
But if you keep on working
and believing,
you'll have victory
in the end.

— *Ann Davies*

I am just beginning
to make some definite changes
in my life.
Some of them will take time,
some will cause me grief,
some will mean risk
and a lot of growing pains, too.
But whatever the case,
I know I will make it...

It's having someone like you
to see me through
both the good times
and the bad
that makes me so sure.

— *Gail Nishimoto*

The only way to find rainbows
is to look within your heart;
the only way to live fairy tales
is through the imagination
and power of your mind;
the only place to begin
a search for peace
is within your very soul;
because rainbows,
fairy tales, and peace
are treasures that grow
from the inside out.

— *Evelyn K. Tharp*

This life is yours
Take the power
to choose what you want to do
and do it well
Take the power
to love what you want in life
and love it honestly
Take the power
to walk in the forest
and be a part of nature
Take the power
to control your own life
No one else can do it for you
Take the power
to make your life
healthy
exciting
worthwhile
and very happy

— *Susan Polis Schutz*

If you have a dream
alive in your mind,
Bring it to the world, give it life.
Too often, the treasures that are
ours alone to give
are never given the chance to grow.
We each have a unique gift
to bring to this world.
It is our purpose in life
to offer this gift.
For even if only a few people
benefit from our offering,
the world is then a better place
to live.

— *Susan Staszewski*

My Prayer...

That I will have the strength
to carry on,
the patience to try again
when things go wrong,
the ability to see beauty
where others see none.
That I will have the hope
of a new dream
waiting to be dreamed,
the chance to reach out,
and the wisdom to look forward
to tomorrow.

— Donna Wayland

Hold fast your dreams!
Within your heart
Keep one still, secret spot
Where dreams may go,
And, sheltered so,
May thrive and grow
Where doubt and fear are not.
O keep a place apart,
Within your heart,
For little dreams to go!

We see so many ugly things —
Deceits and wrongs and quarrelings:
We know, alas! we know
How quickly fade
The color in the west,
The bloom upon the flower.
The bloom upon the breast
And youth's blind hour.
Yet keep within your heart
A place apart
Where little dreams may go,
May thrive and grow.
Hold fast — hold fast your dreams!

— *Louise Driscoll*

Love Your Life

We cannot
listen to what
others want us
to do
We must listen
to ourselves
Society
family
friends
mates
do not know what
we must do
Only we know
and only we
can do what is
right for us
So start
right now
You will need to
work very hard

You will need to
overcome many obstacles
You will need to go
against the better
judgment of many people
and you will need to
bypass their prejudices
But you can have
whatever you want
if you
try hard
enough
So start right now and
you will live
a life designed
by you and
for you
and you will
love
your
life

— *Susan Polis Schutz*

Life is a series of
beginnings...
that bring us closer
to the realization of
our dreams.

May all your
beginnings
be showered by sunbeams
and all your dreams
sense the warmth
of success.

— Edith Schaffer Lederberg

A dreamer lives for eternity.

— Anonymous

For a Happy Life...

Believe in yourself
but don't be overconfident;
Be satisfied
but know that you can always improve;
Accept love graciously
and always be ready to give more;
Be modest in victory and success
and courageous in defeat;
Give comfort and security to others
and you will always receive it in return;
Be glad... just for being
the wonderful person that you are.

— *Lee Wilkinson*

Set yourself earnestly
to see what you are made to do,
and then set yourself earnestly
to do it...
and the loftier your purpose is,
the more sure you will be
to make the world richer
with every enrichment
of yourself.

— *Phillips Brooks*

Deep within our hearts,
each of us carries the seed
of a secret dream,
special and unique to each individual.
Sometimes another person
can share that dream
and help it grow to fulfillment;
other times, the dream remains
a solitary pursuit, known only
to the seeker. But secret or shared,
no matter what it might be,
a dream is a potential which
should never be discouraged. For
each of us also carries within ourselves
a light which can cause the seed
to grow and blossom into beautiful reality...
that same light I've seen shine
so clearly in you.

— *Edmund O'Neill*

The courage of working for
something you believe in,
day in and day out,
year after year,
can be difficult
but holds the greatest rewards.

Find your ideal...
and follow it.

— *V. Sukomlin*

Be All that You Can Be

Champion the right to be yourself.
Dare to be different
and to set your own pattern;
Live your own life,
and follow your own star.

— *Lin Yutang*

If You Think You Can, You Can

Your mind is your real self —
your real being.
There are more and more possibilities in nature,
in the elements, in man and out of man;
and they come as fast as man sees
and knows how to use these forces,
in nature and in himself.

Possibilities and miracles
mean the same thing.

— *Prentice Mulford*

We grow great by dreams.
Dreamers... see things
in the soft haze of a spring day,
or in the red fire
of a long winter's evening.
Some of us let these great dreams die,
but others nourish and protect them,
nurse them through bad days
till they bring them to
the sunshine and light
which comes always to those
who sincerely hope that
their dreams
will come true.

— *Woodrow Wilson*

Today, we share
words and beginnings,
hopes and songs,
expectations for the future —
built from yesterday,
built from now.

Tomorrow...
watercolors and rainbows,
impressions and soft scenes,
a tapestry of feelings —
weaved from memories,
weaved from dreams.

— *Albert M. Ward*

Just as no one can
tell you how to feel
about a beautiful sunset,
no one can tell you how
to live your life.
You are the artist...
and must shape your
experiences
with your own hand.

— *Susan Staszewski*

We can do
anything we want to
if we stick to it
long enough.

— *Helen Keller*

Follow your dreams
and pursue them with courage
for it is the pursuit
of those dreams
that makes life
really worth living.

— *Linda DuPuy Moore*

I dream of beauty
that transcends time
in a world that knows
nothing else
Where all is clean and pure
and good
and all mankind is willing
to help one another
Where discovery is a way of life
and there is no fear of failure
Where God is a very personal
thing that is real to everyone
I dream of a time that has
no pain
and where there is no despair
Where love has a constant meaning
that keeps people together forever
I dream that all this could
someday be true
and I pray that I will share
it all
with you

— *Johnnie Rosenauer*

Let every day
be a dream
we can touch.

Let every day
be a love
we can feel.

Let every day
be a reason
to live.

— *Claudia Adrienne Grandi*

I believe that we cannot live better
than in seeking to become
still better than we are.

— *Socrates*

Don't waste precious time
worrying about
what you should have done...
But rather, focus your attention
on what you are doing now,
and what you want to do
in the future
Don't concentrate
on any mistakes that might
have been made,
but learn from them.

— *Debbie Avery*

A thing
that you
sincerely
believe in
cannot
be wrong.

— *D. H. Lawrence*

The best of life
is that which
ever reaches upward
and strives toward
better things.

— *James R. Miller*

If it should happen
that your dreams
are shattered,
do not be afraid.
Have the courage
to pick up the pieces
and smile at the world.
For dreams that are
easily shattered
can just as easily
be rebuilt.

— *Chris Jensen*

Find happiness in nature
in the beauty of a mountain
in the serenity of the sea
Find happiness in friendship
in the fun of doing things together
in the sharing and understanding
Find happiness in your family
in the stability of knowing
that someone cares
in the strength of love and honesty
Find happiness in yourself
in your mind and body
in your values and achievements
Find happiness in
everything
you
do

— *Susan Polis Schutz*

I like you...
You feel life way down inside.
You have the courage to think
and the strength to get
involved.
You are a dreamer...
and dreamers are too rare...
For few people believe
enough to dream.

— *Linda S. Smith*

I wish for you to
be happy,
and to reach
for the best...
for what is happiness,
if not to believe in
and follow
one's dream?

— *Theophile Gautier*

It's natural to feel disappointed
when things don't go your way
It's easy to think...
"I can't do it, so why try?"
But no matter how scared you are
of making a mistake
or how discouraged you may become,
never give up...
because if you don't try and
if you don't go after what you
want in life,
it won't come to you,
and you'll be forced to accept
things that you know could
be better...

Success is not measured by
whether you win or
whether you fail —
there's always a little bit
of success, even if things
don't go your way —
What's important is that you'll
feel better about yourself,
for the simple reason
that you tried.

— amanda pierce

If you know
who you are and
what you want and
why you want it
and if you have
confidence in yourself and
a strong will to obtain your desires and
a very positive attitude
you can make
your life
yours
if you ask

— *Susan Polis Schutz*

One day at a time —
this is enough.
Do not look back
and grieve over the past,
for it is gone;
and do not be troubled
about the future,
for it has not yet come.
Live in the present,
and make it so beautiful
that it will be worth
remembering.

— *Ida Scott Taylor*

There is a funny old saying that says,
"If you don't ride a bicycle,
you don't fall off!"
What it means to say, of course, is that
if you do put a lot of energy into something,
you are bound to make mistakes;
and if you take a lot of risks,
you are bound to tumble here and there.
But remember this: if you persist,
you will arrive at the destination of your choice.
And if you do occasionally fall in the process,
you'll learn much more than if you don't.

So try, and do, and discover all that you can be.

And take me with you...
in spirit, as you go,
so you'll know that
I'll always be beside you
wishing for nothing but the best.

— *Michael Rille*

In
your moment of success —
I wish for you
a greater mountain to climb,
a wider sea to sail,
a more profound challenge to meet —
for it has been
the journey to the summit,
the reaching for distant shores,
the tenacity to answer the call
that has made you
the most special person you are today.

— *Kele Daniels*

Don't ever give up your dreams...
and never leave them behind.
Find them; make them yours,
and all through your life,
cherish them,
and never let them go.

— *Elisa Costanza*

You Deserve the Best

A person will get only what he or she wants
You must choose your goals carefully
Know what you like
and what you do not like
Be critical about what you can do well
and what you cannot do well
Choose a career or lifestyle that interests you
and work hard to make it a success
Enter a relationship that is worthy of everything
you are physically and mentally
Be honest with people, help them if you can
but don't depend on anyone to make life easy
or happy for you
Only you can do that for yourself
Strive to achieve all that you like
Find happiness in everything you do
Love with your entire being
Make a triumph
of every aspect
of your life

— *Susan Polis Schutz*

Reach for the Stars, Go for Your Dreams!

There are rainbows and pots of gold waiting for you over the horizon, surprises and gifts and wonders just around every corner. Look forward to them. Love them. Catch these pieces of life as they come, and hold them close to you. Savor every moment, every triumph, and even every failure. Don't be afraid to be too passionate to enjoy the ride, chase every quest, and praise every hint of answers to your questions. Dream big. Work hard. Enjoy your play time. Deal with all the challenges in life like the true champ you are. You may not always get what you want, but you're never a failure if you give it your all and do the best you can.

You don't have to be perfect or the smartest person in the world to dream. You don't have to have all the answers or know everything to make your dream come true. Dreams are free, but they belong to the dreamer who'll take a chance.

So let your imagination take you to that perfect place where there is nothing to be afraid of and you can have anything you want. Prepare yourself. Knock on the door of opportunity, and be ready when it answers. Celebrate all the possibilities. Your future is full of hope and happy times, fantasies, and lessons to learn. Learn them well. Enjoy each one. Be good. Believe in miracles. Believe that all things are possible. Love and allow yourself to be loved. Reach for the stars and go for your dreams.

— *Donna Fargo*